AF269036

Sex, Love, Money and then God

Sex, Love, Money

and then God

Betty Jones

Copyright © 2021 by Betty Jones.

Library of Congress Control Number: 2021906737

PAPERBACK: 978-1-955347-90-7
EBOOK: 978-1-955347-91-4

All rights reserved. No part of this publication may be reproduced, distributed, or transmitted in any form or by any electronic or mechanical means, without the prior written permission of the publisher, except in the case of brief quotations embodied in critical reviews and certain other noncommercial uses permitted by copyright law.

Ordering Information:

For orders and inquiries, please contact:
1-888-404-1388
www.goldtouchpress.com
book.orders@goldtouchpress.com

Printed in the United States of America

CONTENTS

ACKNOWLEDGEMENT AND THANK YOU

First I would like to thank God our Lord and Savior Jesus Christ for all the Glory belongs to him. And for the many gifts and many talents that he has blessed me with.

To my wonderful husband Shep Lamar Jones Sr of 36 years you are my strength my provider and pusher, you are always reminding me never to give up but keep the faith and believe that God will see me through the end and God will provide. Love you always.

To my daughter Lillian Bailey you have become my spiritual lion. I love you for the boldness you have become, also thank you for allowing me to use your picture and for your support in the years. My Son Dominique Jones thank you also for your picture and thank you for all your support and strength through the last couple the years of typing this book .You taught me a lot how to use a computer you have help me many times when I press the wrong button and panic. I remember one day streaming Dominique I lost my book I press the wrong button, you came along and press one key my whole book pop back up. Thank you for your patient with me son. My daughter Denise Hollingsworth girl you are my hidden secret of truth strength in a woman. Continue to stay strong in the Lord. Thank y'all.

To my Papa Willie Adams you have taught me that in God all things are possible to keep the faith regardless of what the devil may throw at you. God gets the last say. Things and family may leave you but God will always be with you. I honored you and I will always be grateful for you showing me what true leadership, belief and faith really are, Thank you.

To my Editor Tenishia Toussiant you are my angel sent by God, I thank you for answering the call. For years I prayed for an editor that understand my writing and won't take away what God has given me as a writer. I have hired many editors. But when God sent me Sister Tenishia Toussiant! I knew you were my answered prayer. I love you for your patience with me, for your support and guildness. I look forward to what God is going to do in the future .Again I love you girl. You are the best ever!

DEDICATION

My mother Lillie Dawson Adams

To my mother Lillie Adams you are the best and greatest mother a daughter could ever have., you taught me all that I know as a woman, mother, daughter and sister, when I wanted to give up and throw in towel in my marriage you always told me God will fix everything in my marriage seek him for all my needs. You always prayed and sang your way out, I have learn to pray and sang my way out also .Mama you are the lady who is keeping all us together in this book . I will always remembered your favorite songs walk with me lord and this old building keep on leaning , I will always remember you as a strong woman who believe that God will bring you out of it all. I pray your voice be heard in this book. Mama you are truly miss I hope to see you one day love always your daughter.

INTRODUCTION

CHAPTER 1
SEX, LOVE, MONEY AND GOD

The people in this biography will deal with four subjects within their lives as we do in our own. They are Sex, Love, Money and God.

SEX: Sex is for two in matrimony, in the name of God. However, that is not always the case, it can and sometimes becomes an addiction and this will lead to lust, unfaithfulness to your spouse or partner. It is a very strong emotion and can become a problem. Sex is an emotional and physical need, it is always an issue in our everyday lives. For some of us, our own gender, male or female, will cause a lot of problems we cannot handle on our own. Sex will drive people to do crazy things. Obsession being one in particular. But they fail to realize it until it is too late, for some they aren't aware of what they are doing. They are in denial. As you read on into this book, you will see sex become very heated and we will mention sexual contact.

LOVE: Love is a very strong emotion and also very strong in word. It is always a problem. Some give true love without hesitation or question. We can never understand the question of: Why love is so strange? Why do we put up with so many obstacles in our own relationships? Is love, lust, or your own human desires? We will find out something about ourselves. So read the book ...but wait a minute, not yet!

MONEY: THE LOVE OF <u>MONEY IS THE ROOT OF ALL EVIL!</u> When we use it the wrong way it becomes the evil root, we were sure it would solve all our problems enough to take care of all the debts and some extra on the side to play with. -The All

American Dream!!! HaHaHa, isn't that something to laugh about? Some of us go to work five, six or seven days a week, eight or ten hours daily and still don't seem to get out of the hole!!! Work and pay the bills, love our spouses and our children and would like them to want for nothing, would like them in nice clothes, living in a nice house, with enough food to eat and some things called luxuries. Let's not forget vacations, even if it is not so far from home, the next town even. Yes, money helps us pay our tithes to the church but that is an offering to GOD ALMIGHTY!!! Sometimes, life fails us and we turn to the evil monster, not realizing where we are going and how or why we are doing what we are doing. That green object they call money is the root, we feel there's not enough and we need more. Money will cause you to lie, kill, steal and destroy all of the good things around you. Also hurt those who love you and are the closest to you. It will cause you to do something you would never do, for jingle in your pocket.

GOD: GOD, THE ALMIGHTY ONE, IS WONDERFUL! God, the man with all the plans. We need to think why we call on him when we are in a bind or not until everything is over and done with. We only seem to think we can do things all on our own with no one's help, but it don't work that way. When we get into a bind we call on his help but in the wrong way by asking him: If you can just help get me out of this, just this one time I will......, Jesus, where are you? Well open the book and see why. This Book is about . Maybe, it will shed light on life's issues we all are going and will continue to go through and we grow. And if you haven't seen that light at the end... GOD BLESS YOU AND YOURS! Prayer for y'all will be in my heart.

CHAPTER 2
SEWING CLUB

One boiling and muggy summer day, Ms. Louise was holding one of her famous quilting classes at her sewing shop, in the back room of her house. She held two classes a day, one of her classes comprised four ladies and they befriended on another as the classes continued. They soon grew into a family and shared their life stories of trials and tribulations of their relationships. Learning more on the subjects of sex, love, money and God, but finding out more of the dark secrets of how Ms. Louise's husband treats her. While Ms. Louise and Ms. Esther brings out the materials and equipment they are to be using in class. The young ladies strike up a conversation while sitting at the table, each with their own materials in hand and working on their quilt pieces.

Kendra asks Mimie, "Where is your husband?" Looking sad, Mimie replied, "I don't know, he said he was coming home today, but I haven't heard from him." Kendra said, "I hope he's not burning his wood at both ends!" Joanna interrupts, "Hey! Don't be putting any bad ideas in her head. Can't you see she is very pregnant! Mimie need nothing like sex, money or love on her mind right now." Kendra says, "Well, I'm telling y'all the truth, the man is never home. I remember when my brother was coming home every two or three days, but nine months later, we get a knock at the door. There was a young lady with a babe in arms, telling us the babe was my brothers." Joanna answers, "Oh hush! Your brothers seem to be nothing but hoes!" Ms. Louise frowns and says, "Don't say those words in here! Honey, don't let the ladies bring doubt in you heart about your husband." Patting her on the back. "Baby, does he still send the home to you? Meme answers with her head down, "Yes." Ms. Louise says, "Ok then, that's all that count." Kendra says, "Girl....When the money stops, take yourself and go straight to the health department and lock it all up!" She saunters away to plant herself in a chair. Joanna gasps and says, "Oh my God! I can't believe you! This is a married woman you are talking to, show respect for her and her husband."

Kendra moves her are to sweep the room and says, "Look around you, we got three married woman in here, not counting Paulina." She points at Paulina then continues, "One of her marriages didn't work out because all she wanted was his money and sex. Woman like her, men need to run away from and don't look back or give a second thought!" Paulina answers, "Oh hell no! You back up off out of my business and leave it alone!" Kendra turns and says, "Girl, you bark every time you hear the truth." Mimie says, "Hush now. Will y'all please just change the subject, talk about something else. I am feeling sick, this baby's flipping around."

Joanna looks at the two and says, "Look what you done now, the woman is feeling sick." Putting down her piece and going to Mimie's side. Ms. Louise looking concerned goes over to her and says, "Baby, go get you some water." speaking to Mimie. The front door opens and Ms. Louise's son enters and says, "Hello ladies! Mama? What time will you close?"

Ms. Louise replies: "At nine."

Paulina: "Damn, I wish you were a few years younger!"

Son: "Miss Paulina, I don't like cougars. I got a girl and I love her to death."

Kendra (Laughing out loud): "You got turned down! Go on brother, with your bad self."

Son: "Of man, y'all are crazy!" kisses his mama. "Love you. See you when I get home."

Everybody: "Awww!!!! That's sweet! Mamas' baby." (he walks out the door, closing it behind him.

Ms. Louise looks at Kendra: "Kendra, if you commit adultery, you lack sense and are destroying your own soul."

Kendra replies: "Dang, Mrs. Louise, why you want to call out my name? I had hush on the marriage thing about Paulina."

Ms. Louise replies: "Kendra, it's something about you that makes me curious."

Kendra shouts, and throws her hands in the air: "Oh God! Why do you say that!?"

Ms. Louise shrugs her shoulders while saying: "Oh, I don't know. Maybe, it's those brothers of yours that have you thinking you are tough and invincible."

Paulina interrupts while sitting at the table and sewing together some of her quilt pieces: "We are trying to get somewhere today. Oh Yeah, Ms. Louise what were you saying about your husband yesterday?"

Ms. Louise recalls her conversation of the day before. "Oh yes, the devil tried to get me to commit adultery. If I would've done that, it would be just like I denied my God to his face. This adultery spirit was so heavy on me, the devil was doing whatever he could to make me fail. I had my reasons not to give up and give in, went through this ordeal in my mind daily, but to no avail how to rid myself of these lustful spirits, would pray day and night for strength, would hear words like the way of a fool, are right in his eyes. (Sound of the sewing machines running while she speaks).

Paulina answers: "I tell you after having all these men in my life, somebody would have gotten a phone call. If you know what I mean!"

Kendra smiles and yelling: "Yea, Paulina! Ms. Louise knows what you mean girl! Why, you awful little witch! Anyway, you're not listening to anything Ms. Louise was saying earlier."

Paulina holds up her arm and said: "Dang, I'm listening to it all, but God knows what a woman needs."

Mrs Louise shakes her head while they mock at each other. My God!

This girl needs prayer bad!

Paulina laughs and says: "Kendra, you remember when Ms. Louise said she has never been with another man other than her husband since she was seventeen. Now, she is saying she's feeling strange."

Kendra: "I don't believe it, but ok."

Joanna: "Can't you see what Mrs. Louise is going through? I can't even imagine myself being married to a man for that long, and have an urge to have my husband beside me. To make matters worse, she craves to hold him in her arms and I am by him! It's deep when you crave for someone in that way!"

Paulina holds her stomach and shouts, "Ummm, pizza is my favorite food. I remember when I was pregnant with Michael. Lord have mercy on me. I wanted pizza so bad I tasted it, smelled it; even saw it until I got it. Girl, can you imagine having a man that bad? Hum girlfriend, girlfriend." Kendra speaks with an attitude: "Ok Paulina, I understand. Ms. Louise, what did you do when all this happened?"

CHAPTER 3
THE HEATED MOMENT

Ms. Louise: "Well, my mother was a person that likes to spice things up a little too much. She gave me some good pointers on what to do."

Kendra laughs: "What did she say?"

Mrs. Louise continues: "Well, I called up my husband and told him not to work hard, because I needed him."

Kendra interrupts once again: "What did he say?"

Ms. Louise looks at her and says: "If you would be quiet, I'll tell you. He gave me that little chuckle like always. But when he got home, I was expecting something good as the night progressed. As the tension got more overwhelming, I expressed my desire. As usual, he laughed. At that moment, I felt my emotions explode in my gut. I realized, that he wasn't ready for what I had in store for him. I turned over and cried myself to sleep, because I knew what he was going to say, I was not trying to hear it. It was like a moment in a slow motion romance movie. He laughed and placed his hands over my waist. I am burning on the inside begging God for his mercy. All of a sudden, his voice sounding like Hurricane Misty on the Mississippi coast. His breathe feeling so cold and chilling, I felt his eyes look at me with a smirk, 'I can't help you.' he replies. I thought to myself, Oh God what am I supposed to do? I wasn't ready for that type of rejection from my own husband!" My heart was beating like King Kong's mighty fist on his chest trying to stay alive. This was the last blow that I could take from him. I felt like giving up, betrayed, deceived and left out in the cold all alone. Deep down inside I was crying to God that the world was over, I felt so empty and lost. My husband was everything to me and my life was centered on him, even though he wasn't what I wanted him to be. I will love him no matter what happens between us, but this rejection just tore me apart and totally hurt me to no end. I continue to pray, always asking God. Is it just lust that my flesh desires?"

Paulina: "Hold on now! Don't you go feeling sorry for yourself? My God, that couldn't have been me. I would have been on the phone calling up one of my boys and called it a night of real lovemaking. Mrs. Louise, you just don't know how much fun me and my wood can have when the heat is on. (with an attitude).

Mrs. Louise shakes her head once again: "I told you that child needs to be prayed for. Go get my oil and let me anoint you. Not just your head, but your whole body."

Paulina stands up and walks around looking like she's eager to speak and says: "I tell you what. Whatever is good for the goose is good for the gander."

Kendra looks at her in disgusting rage and replies: "Paulina, I'm glad Mrs. Louise didn't know you when she was going through all that."

At the same time Paulina trying to talk and laugh. "Girl, all you would have had to do was call me and one of my baby daddy's could help you out."

Kendra frowns while saying, "Oh my God, you are so nasty! No wonder you don't have a real man.

Paulina looks at her speaks with attitude, "Oh you didn't know? When a man finds a woman, he finds a good thing."

Kendra drops her head while saying, "Don't you ever think before you talk? You said a woman, and that (snaps her finger) you are not. So it's obvious, that doesn't apply to you."

Paulina stood up and says, "Who are you talking to like that? Somebody better make this dog stop barking and go lay her down before I do. Anyway bark when someone is on your own property! We got this boo!"

Kendra: "Oh! I know you are not calling me a dog."

Ms. Louise replies, "Ladies, let's get back on what we were talking about."

In the midst of all of that commotion, Ms. Ester was just looking and silently praying for the both of them. She looks around and starts back, "Yes dear, shall we?"

Kendra started asking Ms Louise again, "So your husband turned you down in the midst of a heated moment?"

Mrs. Louise answers, "He sure did. Like I was saying earlier, he crushed my heart. I was so emotional all I could do was cry. Once he told me that he couldn't help me, I ran straight to the bathroom, I spent all night in there crying. I cried so hard that my eyes were similar to a boxer after a twelve round fight. Over and over again, I felt very light headed. I was burning up like God was holding a magnifying glass to my heart. The heat of passion was on, but on the outside, I felt like I was losing my mind. This was the first time I ever felt like that. Let me tell you this, the feeling that I have for my husband is the most painful feeling ever. This situation goes to show you that we all think differently. Loving a person is not easy when they don't love you back. It's very hard being in love alone.

Joanna, "While listening to you I am learning everyday."

Ms. Louise, "You can have sex by yourself. I found out the next day that almost all the woman that was around me was having sex with there new piece. I learned about all kinds of sex toys that I didn't know existed. People all around me was using these toys like using a man or woman. I had one of my associates advised me to go home and get dressed, like I was going on a real date. Stop by the toy store and buy a penis larger than my husband."

Mimie: "That's just nasty!" (All the ladies look, hum, and snap their fingers. I'm gonna keep my wood.

Ms. Louise: "Anyway, my associate told me to take my penis toy out for dinner and talk to my penis, let him know we are going to the best hotel after dinner, and don't forget to get the energizer rechargeable batteries, and to have a good time with my man guaranteed never to fail."

Joanna: "Now Ms. Louise, don't you know that lady was messed up in the head? Hell, Ms. Louise I love my wood."

Kendra: "This time I agree, y'all give me the real deal. Go buy you a good hoe dog first. Ladies, a hoe dog? What in the world is that?"

Ms. Ester laughed: "Ok ladies, we know sex without a man is not safe or good. There are men and woman out there who will fulfill our needs. We don't have to settle for anything less. Ladies lets get this last block in and go home. We have heard enough.

CHAPTER 4
THE TWO FUSSERS

The very next day they all come back to the sewing class and are going to start on a new quilt. Some of the conversation from the night before surfaces and then at this point Kendra looks very interested in the conversation.

Paulina starts to speak.

Kendra cuts her off, "We already know. You would just call up one of you baby daddies, or a cake daddy friend. Like always, they will have fixed the entire problem. How about you not talk for a minute? This isn't the time for that and your solutions won't help anything. You are just awful, uh! So Mrs. Louise, what caused your husband to even say he's not ready?"

Ms. Louise answers, "Well while we were in the middle of our greatest trial involving our daughter, things that I thought were buried had come back up. The stale attitude that I used to dread had come back. I heard the word say, 'when the spirit leaves the body, it goes to find a place to rest. If they can't find a place, they will come back to you if they find you empty. This time when they come back, they will stay seven times worse than what they were before they departed.' I was a victim to that exact thing."

Kendra interrupts, "Ms. Louise, what happened?"

Ms. Louise answered, "My husband did a lot of fighting."

Kendra's mouth dropped, "Oh Lord, please don't tell me that he hit you?"

Ms. Louise shakes her head, "Yes, Kendra, he has done it several times throughout our marriage, and it caused us to break up. Let me tell you why we got into it. One night, it was really hot and I got up to go turn on the air conditioner. He doesn't like for the air to be turned up too high, which I can understand, because he is the one paying the bill. It was so stuffy that I could `barely catch my breath. He came storming into the living room making a scene about how he pays the bills and everyone was going to suffer with the heat or leave his house. When he said that, all hell broke loose and my life was never the same. My husband had a totally different mind frame when it came to our marriage. That night I truly saw death in his eyes. He was not the man that I agreed to marry."

Kendra replies to Ms. Louise, "Good God Ms. Louise, you have gone through the fire." She jumps up and shouts, "If a man ever put his hands on me. I will do him in!"

CHAPTER 5
THE MONSTER WITHIN

Kendra with a raging attitude, "My God, I feel steam right now! Lord God! Pleeeease cool me down, woo! How do you say it, Ms. Esther? JESUS! I need you now, because if her husband walks in this house I'd probably do something to him."

Paulina feeling sad says to Kendra, "Calm down, Let Ms. Louise finish. What happened that night?"

Ms. Louise gets comfortable on her couch and looks around, as if she could see everything like yesterday. She began to speak, "Well, he came at me with his drinking mug in hand, with the intention of hitting me. My daughter started screaming and all I was focused on was the mug. My daughter screamed, 'No daddy! Don't you hit my mama! I'm tired of you treating her like this. You need to go somewhere and chill out!" The next thing I knew, the mug was hitting the wall, the bedroom door was slammed, and my husband was in the room fussing to himself, until he dozed off."

Amazed at the story, Kendra says, "My God, you went through pure hell with that guy, huh?"

Ms. Louise answered saying, "Child, I sure did! I knelt down and prayed for protection and strength to go on with my life. My husband knew I would press charges and have him arrested, he then threatened our lives and told me not to do that. I agreed, just to protect us at that time. As much as I hated to do it, the next morning I went on a stroll looking for a safe place to stay for us. God was looking out for us, I found that safe abode the very same day! I took my family there and we stayed for about sixty days. The good part about the new place is we practically lived for free at the hotel. It was God's favor that was with us through it all. Soon, the time came for us to return back home. I consulted with my lawyer and she told me there was a way to bypass my husband and get back into my house. All I wanted to do was get my children back home.

With a concerned look Mimie asks Ms. Louise, "What did you do? I want to know, just in case I have to go that route one day.

Ms. Louise looks at Mimie and answers, "Child, I hope you don't, but you have a very good husband. My family was in danger, since my husband had been classified as an abuser. So by law, the Women's Shelter provided protection for us. I filed for a divorce, but I was informed that I needed to file for a legal separation first. So with the legal papers I filed against him I will gain full access to my home and it was stated in these papers, he would have to take care of the mortgage payments and the child support of $480.00. Within the legal papers there was also a 100ft restraining order in place.

My husband was court ordered out of the house and escorted by the police out of the neighborhood. After all this madness had taken place, I received a phone call from the Women Protective Services, informing me that it was safe to return home. To my surprise he didn't take any of his clothes. I had to meet him in a Plaza so I could give his clothes to him.

As he stood there looking sad he started saying with his heart and eyes full of tears, "Honey I don't believe you would do something like this to me, you bust a hole in my heart! (sniffling and wiping his face). You brought the law into our marriage, which is something that I despise. You know I hate the police. If I see them walking on the street I will spit on them! (Lord God, help this man!) Honey, I hope I never see that judge on the street. It's going to be me and him!

Kendra looks up in awe, "My God, Ms. Louise, you took all of this just to keep your children drama free. Your husband had some major problems.

Ms. Louise, "Well, he didn't see it that way! In the midst of that particular trial, he fell into the traps of the streets at the age of 51. From that point on, the situation got worse and while he was in the streets, he started to partying, drinking heavily, hitting the clubs and he met new friends of all kind. They all hung out together getting closer by the second. He would even lie and say he wasn't involved with anyone but he gave himself away when he came home with sob stories, 'baby I'm sorry role. Please let me come home. I love you there's no one else but you.' I knew he was telling me a lie. I could literally see the other woman all over his face and I could feel her in his spirit. I felt so strong about it that I asked him and he said, "Naw, honey, I love you." I would try to believe him, but deep down inside and I just couldn't, so I blew off every word! We had been separated for a year, but it seemed like a lifetime, even though he was in and out visiting the children wanting to stay with us but I wouldn't allow him to. He was still in denial about having someone else. A lot of people tried to convince me that my husband wasn't having an affair.

Kendra interrupts once again, you mean to tell me that 'Mr. Too Slick' is showing all evidence that he is as guilty as a junkyard dog prowling in a trash for a bone. Why couldn't he be a man about the thing and just tell the truth? Instead he wants you to fall for that sad love story. Hahaha. He best think again! Negro please! Here you are sitting at home in heat like a lonely puppy. He sitting his sad self up there talking about I can't help you. We see why he can't help you because he is out and about giving your goods to charity and the rest of the hood!"

Paulina had nodded off earlier during the conversation but has awoken and despairingly says, "Kendra girl, will you please hush! Do more listening and less talking from now on. Dear God, I don't see how you can take it. I really don't see it."

Kendra raises her voice, "You don't see because you aren't listening to what she's saying either, with you being over there knocked out. I just wish a fly would've landed in your mouth! Anyway, you go on and continue Ms. Louise."

Ms. Louise takes a sip from her coffee. She sits up in her chair and says, "With all that said and done, after three years of trials and tribulations, my husband was still holding on to his bad habits. I had begun to have even more faith in God. With all of this mess going on, Mrs. Esther, encouraged me to hold on to my marriage.

Mimie is sitting in an overstuffed chair in the corner with an astonished look on her face rubbing on her tummy and all the while listening to Ms. Louise's story. She comments, "Wow, that's spooky Ms. Louise, after all of that drama you wasn't scared?'

Ms. Louise replied, "No, but if I didn't know no better, I believe I wouldn't have gone to meet him. Yes indeed girl I would've been so scared my shell would have crumbled! However, the actions of my husband took the fear out of me and with the help of God it made me stronger."

Mimie answers, "I've only been married for a few and can't even imagine myself going through something like you have, Ms. Louise."

CHAPTER 6
LIFE WOULD NEVER BE THE SAME

After all the ladies have eaten lunch in the kitchen, they return to the sewing room and resume with the making of the new quilt. The conversation is continued by Ms. Louise.

Ms. Louise, "I had hope that life would give me a fresh start after continually battling with my desires. I felt neglected while my husband's needs were being met. He continued to do what he did for a very long time. Every time I would ask him where he had been, he would say out with his friends. That was a lie, because I still could see that same nasty woman all over him. My famous saying came to pass when I said, 'Time will tell.' Meanwhile, I'm asking God to help me and don't let me fail. I was battling the spirit of loneliness, the need of a sexually companion, and for that comfort all over again. Everything that the devil had to offer, he threw it at me."

In the meantime, it had started to storm as Mrs. Louise ends her conversation about her life, with her husband.

Kendra noticed how late it was getting and replies, "Oh Ms. Louise, I believe we need to be on our way home now."

Mrs. Louise looks her way and responds with dismay, "Why do you have to leave now? I'm just getting started!"

Kendra looks towards the window again and points, "Look it's storming outside, not only that, it's hailing also. My God, I hope we make it home safe."

Mrs. Louise shakes her head and looks up at Kendra and says, "Now you know you are going to get home alright. The Lord has already dispatched his angels to watch over you as you go home. Don't be afraid of the Lord's' work."

Paulina replies by saying, "Okay ladies it's getting a bit noisy outside, I think it is time to go before something happens." But just as Paulina finishes her sentence there is a loud noise.

Kendra runs to the window shouting, "Look! Lightning has just struck a tree limb nearby!" All the ladies ran to the window and looked out in concern.

Paulina responds, "For real I'm going to go and see how big it is!"

Ms. Louise looks at Paulina with a weird look saying, "I don't know child, from the sound of things that was a pretty big tree limb.

Besides its storming nobody needs to be out there right now."

Mimie chimes in and says, "Yeah, for real girl! I don't like traveling in storms like this. I'm going to the house."

Paulina says, "Hey girl, I'm going to the house too!"

Ms. Louise looks around at everyone and says, "Jesus!"

Mimie comes back after retrieving her coat. She waves and says, "Ladies, I'll see you all tomorrow, if not then, this weekend. I just might call you on the phone instead, I was not feeling good today, it's probably something I ate."

Paulina tilts her head and says, "Mimie take your time, believe it or not that baby will be in this world before you know it!"

Mimie laughs and says, "Ok Paulina! I am counting down my days." Boom! Boom! Boom! (thunder), lightning lights up the room.

Kendra finally speaks after a long moment following the sounds, "Oh my God! Did you all hear that thunder?"

Mimie starts to breathe hard, grabs her chest and then her stomach, then responds while covering her ears, "See.... that's why I'm on my way home. If I hear another sound that loud, I will be having this baby in this here house!"

Paulina looks at Mimie in concern and says, "Yeah you go home, we be alright."

Ms. Esther speaks, "Mimie, I pray that Isaiah will be home with you on that blessed day. He works so hard at his job, driving those trucks on those long hauls.

Mr. Louise comes back and says, 'Oh, Ms. Esther do not start me talking again!" Everyone laughs, while Meme is looking disappointed.

Mimie says, "I really need to go home. Without you all I don't know what I'd do. Praising God is the only thing I can do right now, especially with Isaiah on the road all the time."

Ms. Louise points and replies, "Now don't you start complaining child, he's making that money that's all that counts right now. Am I right?"

Mimie smiles and continues, "Yes ma'am, you are right."

Ms. Louise speaks on behalf of everyone, "Mimie we understand you need all your rest after the baby is born.

Mimie continues speaking as she walks toward the door, "Ok you all, this time I am going on to the house, talk to you all later." Mimie leaves.

Everyone shouts, "We Love you Mimie, see you later, and drive safe!"

Paulina speaks, "Ok Ms. Esther, I guess I'll go too, but I will surely see you tomorrow!"

Ms. Esther replies with a smile, 'Alright Paulina, you drive safe sweetie."

Paulina waves and asks Kendra, (Kendra is sitting with her eyes glued to the TV.) "Kendra, are you riding back with me?"

Kendra looks up from the TV and answers Paulina, "No, I am going to ride back with Keisha, this movie is starting to get good." Kendra asks Ms. Louise, "What time does this movie end?"

Ms. Louise replies while pointing at the remote, "I don't know honey, look at the TV guide and find out."

Kendra looks towards Keisha and asks, "Would you pass me the remote please?" Kendra is checking the time while continuing to watch the movie.

Keisha asks Kendra, "What time does it say, I have to be at work at 6:00, we can't be here no longer then 12.

Kendra answers, "Oh well we straight then, because it's over at 12, so we'll leave then.

Keisha looks at Ms. Esther and asks, "So are you going to spend the night with Ms. Louise to keep her company after that touching story she told us?

Ms. Esther looks up and grins as she says, "Why yes darling!I am just a little old lady trying to make sure you ladies do right, but now Ms. Louise needs my help around here so I am going to stay."

As Keisha looks at her watch, she says, "I hear that. Okay Kendra you only got about 5 more minutes."

Kendra gets up and gets a drink of water and responds, "Alright Keisha, I guess we can leave now." Keisha and Kendra both wave as they go out the door.

Ms. Louise says, "Ok ladies, you all have a safe trip."

They respond happily, "Yes ma'am we'll see you two tomorrow."

Night has come to this small house, with the storm brewing outside.

The two ladies are all alone to themselves and they are starting to settle in for the night.

CHAPTER 7
THE NIGHT IS LONG AND WELL SPENT.

The ladies have all left, Ms. Louise and Ms. Esther gets comfortable and begin to talk in the living room with tea cups in their hand. They have both been in similar ordeals but each dealt with it differently. Now that they are alone, they reflect on the days events and give God Praise.

Ms. Louise sighs and speaks, "Ms. Esther, those ladies just don't know how good God is, do they?"

Ms. Esther laughs, rocking in her chair, sipping on her tea, and says, "Hum they sure don't. I sure can remember those days. When I was young as they are and nothing could phase me. Louise, it may be very hard sometimes to beat this battle. Honey believe me, our God don't put no more, on you then what you can handle. God put us together, for you to be around the power of his anointing. He has given me all the power in this battle you are going through, so you are not alone. You are going to win this battle, in Jesus name. You are a proverbs woman, which is a good woman. God is looking at every step you take." As Ms. Esther is talking to Ms. Louise, she puts her hand on her forehead and starts to cry. Mrs. Esther goes over to console her as she pats her on the back, "Oh Louise, don't cry. Save those wonderful tears for those ladies you are teaching. They are the ones who you need to cry for honey. Can you imagine what other people are going through right now? Somebody needs to hear your testimony, it's the power that you are gaining right now in Jesus name. Honey, most people in your shoes would have given up a long time ago. Can't you see the Holy Spirit is purifying you? Unlike your husband. Whenever you get the craving for him the Holy Spirit takes you to the word. Telling you, when a man finds a woman, he finds a good thing, that's a gift given to you from God. Not all people are blessed like you, to hear God. Many people will love to be able to hear the word just like you do. Louise, you have a lot of wisdom, knowledge and most of all, understanding. The word of God says that we are to get understanding and you have got that. Understand now, when God finishes with you, he will give you the desire of your own heart. Yes, your husband is your most desire, but the word says, a woman is to honor and obey her husband. Your husband may not have the desire but that's alright. You just keep that desire it is helping you to keep your marriage whole. Your mind, body and soul will tell you all kinds of stuff, believe it or not. This is the case where we got to die in the flesh, put it on the cross, pleading to the father not my will, but thy will, will be done. Honey your spirit needs to come alive!" Ms. Esther changes positions as she is startled by Ms. Louise's alarm clock, 'Ring---------Ring!' Ms. Esther says, "What IS that noise?"

Ms. Louise chuckles and says, "Oh that's just my alarm clock. Why, did it startle you?"

Ms. Esther shakes her head with wide eyes and says, "Yes indeed, well gosh if that's what it is, we need to be getting some rest. What time do your sewing classes start?"

Ms. Louise checks out her watch and replies, "Oh around 9 in the morning. It is kind of late, lets try and get some rest."

As they walk towards the bedrooms Ms. Esther asks, "Have you gotten any new girls yet?"

Ms. Louise turns to Ms. Esther while they walk down hall and replies, "Yes ma'am, earlier this week."

Ms. Esther nods in belief and says, "Do you have enough room?"

Ms. Louise answers with a glance towards her bedroom door, "I have plenty of room. I may need to get some more machines."

As they arrived at their rooms Ms. Esther says, "Well, always pray for the power of success. I am going to go in this room and get some rest. Ms. Lady I would say good night, but it will be good morning in a little while. I'll just talk to you later."

Ms. Louise responds as she walks into her room, "Yes ma'am, I'll just let you wake on your own. I Love you, Ms. Esther."

Mr. Esther turns around one last time and says, "I Love you too baby!"

Mrs. Louise goes to lies down, she prays to God for all his will in their lives. As the songs of the radio, set the pleasance of a peaceful night. Her eyes get heavy and she falls sound asleep.

CHAPTER 8
MORNING HAS COME

Morning creeps up on the two as the trash truck passes by, "Zooooom Mmm...mmm! They are rudely awakened out of their peaceful wonderful sleep.

Ms. Louise jumps up by the sound of the trash truck, startled she shouts, Oh my God, I'm late getting up! That sounded like the trash truck going by. I really hope that child took that trash out last night. Ms. Louise looks out the window to see if the trash is on the side of the road. She continues. He sure didn't put it out there like always. Boy, I tell you the truth, you give a child a little rope they'll hang themselves. I sure do hate to wake him, but he needs to get on his job. As she goes to his room, she changes her mind and throws her hands up and walks back to the kitchen. As she takes the trash out, she notices the yard and says to herself. When Dah wakes up he has got to do something to this yard. He knows his daddy don't like nasty yards. That's one of his pet peaves, a nasty yard, so let me tell him before his dad comes to visit. Oh God I don't know why I am still trying to satisfy him like he still live here. [Zooooom Mmmm] "Oh my, the trash men are getting here pretty quick, let me hurry before I miss them!"

"Good morning Ms. Louise!" says a neighbor.

Ms. Louise returns to the yard, she turns around and waves. As she hurries into the house, the phone rings, it stops when she gets to the door. They sure didn't want anything, if it was important they'll call back. Ms. Louise goes to the counter to make coffee while thinking about the goodness of God. While this coffee is getting ready I am going to praise your name! Ms. Louise goes into to high praise, right in her kitchen, 'God I love you. You have been so good to me.' I thank you God for all your blessings and your word that you have given me to stand on each and everyday. For this is the day that the Lord has made, I will rejoice and be glad in this day of prosperity and success. Ooooo and I thank you Jesus for my customers. I pray Lord that their eyes be opened to see how to sew like never before.

Ms. Esther enters the kitchen inhaling the smell of fresh brewed coffee saying, "Hmmmm that sure do smell good. I hear you Louise, in here giving God the glory without me. And you wonder why you are so strong in his presence. As long as you exalted the Lord, you don't have to worry about a thing. The devil can come at you with his whole army of angels, and still couldn't touch you. Ms. Esther stops and looks at Ms. Louise and says with command, "Do you hear me talking to you child?"

Ms. Louise turns and smiles, while coming out of her praise, and reaches down to hug Ms. Esther, she replies, "Yes, ma'am."

Ms. Esther winks and says, "Now hand me that cream and sugar, while I sit and admire this beautiful kitchen setting you got going in here. Do you ever sit and thank God for this big beautiful house you have?"

Ms. Louise sets her coffee down and turns towards Mrs. Esther with gladness saying, "Oh yes ma'am. Some people don't even have a nice house and I do thank my God. Yes indeed, I am truly blessed."

Ms. Esther nods as she sips her coffee. Both of the ladies are enjoying their coffee as Ms. Esther continues, "Honey you said a mouthful a minute ago. Oh child, how is your husband doing this morning? Has he called you yet?"

Ms. Louise looks up to the ceiling and shook her head saying, "Well he hasn't so, I guess he's fine. (Sarcastically, snorting). That hard headed son of ours didn't take the rest of that trash out. He really doesn't like getting up on trash day even though that's his job.

Ms. Esther looks at her with her hands on her hips and scooted her glasses down the bridge of her nose and saying, "Honey you got to stay on those boys, you can't give them any rope, they'll hang themselves every time. My husband is gone to be with the Lord, I loved him to the end. One thing I can say, he raised our seven boys well. Every task he gave them to do, they done with no hesitations. I'm not saying it was easy, but God made it easy. Raising boys is a handful. They will try you with all their might. That's why I thank God. Back in those days, women were housewives, and hard workers, we had more control in those days. We had strong men with a backbone and were able to go out and provide for their families. But nowadays, I don't know what these men got in their backs!" Ms. Louise laughs as Ms. Esther continues, "We had good, dependable, Godly men in our day. They even had the fear of God in them. Our men knew how to love us regardless of what situation we were in at that point in time. My boys to this day are great men of God. Don't get me wrong a few of them have tried to get off track, but prayer brought them back. My husband has been gone a long time now. He did wrong and wallowed in his dirt but prayer changed it all. Lord knows, I have walked in your shoes at one time and was just like you. Ms Esther sat shaking her head, sips the last bit of her coffee and asks Ms. Louise to pour up her some more. "Your sewing class should be starting soon shouldn't it?"

Ringgggg...gg, the phone rings as Ms. Louise heads to the coffee pot. Ms. Esther gets up instead and says, "Honey you answer the phone I'll pour us some coffee."

Ms. Louise responds, "Yes, Ma'am." and answers the phone, "Hello, Reap What You Sow Quilting, how may I help you?"

Mimie asks, "Is this Mr. Louise?"

Ms. Louise shakes her head as if Mimie can see her and says, "Good Morning, how are you doing Mimie?'

Mimie answers, "I'm fine. I was calling to let you know that I am going to be a little late for class. I forgot that I had a Dr. Appointment today."

Ms. Louise smiles and says, "Oh sweetie, you need to go on to the doctor, so that the baby can get checked. We'll be here when you get out. Oh yeah, is your husband going with you?"

Mimie answers disappointedly and says, "No, he's not going this time." Ms. Louise feels the sadness in her voice and says," Now don't 'cha worry baby, he'll be there next time okay? Now you take care and be safe." Ms. Esther looks up, setting the coffee down and asks, "Who was that?

It sounded like that Mimie girl."

Ms. Louise laughs and answers, "Yes ma'am, it was."

Ms. Esther looks at the time and says, "When are those ladies coming in, it's almost 9:00. I want to learn how to sew me a quilt too."

Ms. Louise looks at the clock and says, "They'll be here. Sometimes it's a little slow."

Ms. Esther gives her a puzzled look and says, "Okay, so what do you do when it's slow like this?"

Ms. Louise smiles and replies, "Well most of the time, I pray or study the word of God. I also write down some of my drawings that I use for my teaching."

Ms. Esther nods and says, "Oh, so that's where those instructions come from."

Mrs. Louise chuckles and responds, "Yes ma'am, God will give me the plans every night in my dreams. When I wake up I will write them down and pray over them."

Ms. Esther looks in amazement and says, "Dear God, you and him got it like that."

Ms. Louise nods as she does a little dance and says, "Yes ma'am and I love it that way. I never went to school for what I do, I just consider myself blessed."

Ms. Esther says while waving her hand, "Yes, Yes, Yes it is also called gifted and talented. Don't get me wrong now. I'm not against education now. That's an important thing in life too, but it's just something about that word of God." They both chuckled while Ms. Esther continues and as she looks at her watch again she asks, "Does your husband go to work everyday at the same time?"

Ms. Louise shrugs her shoulders and says, "I guess, I don't know."

Ms. Esther frowns and says, "What do you mean you guess?"

Ms. Louise looks as if she doesn't want to be on this subject, "I mean he seems the same, but I don't know."

Ms. Esther, "Do you know God said we should seek counseling."

Ms. Louise answered, "Yes, and he refused?"

Ms. Esther looks surprise and says, "Really."

Ms. Louise nods her head and continues with a tear in her eye, "Yes ma'am, but he don't care. It wasn't long before he was back in the streets again. I knew in my heart that we needed help. He even lied to get back home. He asked to come and wash clothes and hasn't left here yet. I should have seen that coming. Most of the time we are in each other presence it feels as if somebody or something is coming between us."

Ms. Esther takes a deep breath and says, "Well have you prayed and fasted about that feeling?"

Ms. Louise nods her head as she runs her fingers through her hair and says, 'Yes ma'am, that and a whole lot of other problems that we have."

Ms. Esther adjusts her seat and gets a little more comfortable while saying, "Have you gone to get help for yourself? So what does he do sometimes to make you feel uncomfortable besides sex?"

Ms. Louise looks at Ms. Esther while saying, "I can't even get him to give me a hug, and when I do see him, he is in the fetal position. He gets comfortable on the couch watching football or shall I say football looking at him."

They both chuckle as Ms. Esther says, "Wow! That's a shame. I didn't know it was that bad."

Ms. Louise shakes her head as she says, "Yes ma'am, it is."

Ms. Esther looks in disgust and says, "You know what? I don't mean to scare you, but my one of my friends was telling me, her husband did the same thing to her. Come to find out, he was over there swollen from the two women he had sex with before he got home! So my child, please be wise at what you do with him. There is too much STD going around out there. These men can't hang out like they used, to back in my days. I'm not saying sleeping around is right, but it was safer in my days. These men need to go watch TV or go fishing to get their rocks off. Until they find a good church that will teach them about the word of God so they can have the power to overcome that devil!

Ms. Louise answers, "Yes, I hear you, that's the truth right there! I don't know what kind of love we have for each other these days, but it sure isn't the one that God wants for us!"

Ms. Esther continues, "Lord knows I need my husband right now. So do you think your husband is messing around?"

Ms. Louise, "Yes! You know when I look back on that day, I get the chills as if it just happened."

Ms. Esther looks with concern on her face. She sits there and just tries to imagine what Mrs. Louise is going through, but just can't get that feeling. She doesn't want to go back but she think it's time just to help her out a little. "Ok Louise, I got a few past terrors to tell you and maybe you won't feel so bad or alone. Honey, life hasn't always been peaches and cream. I never told you, my husband was a pastor and a judge. All you know is little old Ms. Esther. Okay my dear while we wait for the ladies to arrive let me tell you a story. Baby, you sit right down there, while I fix us another cup of coffee and let me tell you what I have been through. Ms. Esther inhales the smell of the coffee. God that sure smells good.

CHAPTER 9
THE TRIAL OF MS. ESTHER

The two ladies are still sitting at the kitchen table, drinking coffee and waiting on the girls to arrive for the quilting class.

Ms. Esther starts telling her story to Ms. Louise, "Well, I give God the glory for long term standing power. While we wait on the girls, let me tell you about a bad habit that my husband had. My husband is long gone now, so I'm sure he won't mind. But honey he sure did have some good days and some bad days. There wasn't always water in my pot, and that flower sure didn't bloom."

Ms. Louise, "What do you mean by that?"

Ms. Esther looks at Ms. Louise sadly and replies, "Well my husband like porn flicks, he loved them more then he loved me, I can say that now. There were times when the porn flicks got all the attention and then some. On top of that, I had to act out some of the little tricks in the flicks in order to get my husbands' needs meet." Ms. Esther pauses and takes a sip of coffee and continues. "I never liked this part of my life because I felt he was not loving me, he was in love with what the porno flicks can do for him. Plenty of times, my husband couldn't even perform without the porn flicks. I won't even mention the books that he used to have. The saddest part of it all, I wasn't allowed to touch his movies or books.

Ms. Louise, "Did you touch them?"

Ms. Esther, "Only when I got tired of that flick. I would sneak them out and put them in the trash. I would get punished that night and he would use all the toys in the books or movies that would cause me pain."

Ms. Louise, "Oh my, God, No!"

Ms Esther, "Baby, I knew what you were saying, when you were talking about the toys. Oh yeah, the men have toys too! They have them for their own use. Baby, when I say I have seen and used them all. I have seen and used them, all but the ones they made recently, since my husband died. When he died those toys died too! I took the toys to the grave buried them with him, there was his big black bag next to him in the casket and people wondered what was in that bag. They all thought, him being a judge and a pastor, I was putting some of there hidden sins and evidence in the grave with him. But the devil is a liar! Those were his sins that were never told and I never told anybody to this day, only you. She breathed in and folded her hands as she leaned back in the chair and said, "Baby! There was many a night I prayed that my sons never saw them. A lot of times I would pray for relief. The porn addiction got so bad that I didn't even want to sleep with him, because I knew I would have to act out like one of the girls he saw in the flick or in a smut book. Years went by, and I began to get tired of it, so I started to pray about it. I was getting delivered from wanting to satisfy my husband at any and all cost. I learned that sex doesn't have to be a mimic out of a smut book or porn flick. I learned to stand up for myself and say'NO, I WILL NOT BE YOUR PORN STAR.' I am your wife!"

Ms. Louise asks in shock as to what she is hearing, "Ms Esther, you went through that?"

Ms. Esther replies in anger, "Oh let me tell you the cost I had to pay. That devil sure didn't want to let me go without a fight. The weekends were always our time to spend with one another, but on one weekend my sister and her husband came over to visit us for a while and at that time I was seeking the Lord for deliverance. He was dealing with me about my husband, at this time he was a pastor and a judge. My husband and my brother-in-law went to the store to get some drinks. My sister and I were talking and listening to the music, she asked me if we had any good porn flicks, they can watch.

Ms. Louis asks, "Ms Esther? Which sister are you are talking about? It's not the one that's with you all the time is it?"

Ms Esther exclaims, "Oh no, Hell no! Hell will freeze over if she come to me talking about porn flicks. I swear, I will beat her until she come back to her senses, uhmmmm. If she ever did that, she would be putting shame on my God!"

Ms. Louise asks, "Well have I seen this sister?"

Ms. Esther, "No, I don't think so. You know there is nine of us including marriage? But any way I gave her the very good porns. We had plenty to share so I didn't think nothing of it and then we got the tv, vcr and the magazine."

Ms. Louise jokingly replies, "That's more then enough, Ms Ester. Maybe I should try some porns."

Ms. Esther looking very stern, replies, "And I will beat you silly! You are fine, just the way you are. So I let my sister take the good ones. Hummm, to my memory, I gave her more than enough. She was happy. By then the men had come back from the store. We all sat and drank for a little while. It was happy time the children were gone." She looked at her coffee cup and it was empty. "Honey, pour me some more coffee please, and when you come over here I am going to show you something." Ms, Esther grabs Ms. Louise's hand and says, "Look at my face. Do you see them very dark shallows under my eyes?"

Louise says, "Yes ma'am, are you sleepy?"

Ms. Esther replies, "No I am not."

Ms. Louise asks, "Are you stressed out?

Ms. Esther sadly answers, "No I'm not and it's not old age. Let me tell you what they are. These baby, are old bruises that were left behind and the marrying just never healed, people think its old age, but it's not. Thank God my husband is gone to be with the Lord, because I will not be sitting here talking to you like this. Remember he was a preacher and a judge and no one will believe little old ladies like me. In my days we kept our mouth shut tight. We would not talk about our husbands or nothing that he did, just as long as he brought the money home and did what was right in the eyes of the people. We were to keep quiet and just deal with it. Baby this is how we learn early how to pray. I know many ladies who been through the storm and they took it all to the grave. Honey, we are in different times now and y'all are so blessed and got so much freedom." (tears roll down her cheeks).

Ms. Louise goes over to Ms. Esther and comforts her, letting her know, she is not alone. Ms. Esther sniffles for awhile and calms down enough to continue their conversation.

Ms. Louise asks, "So what happened to your sister?"

Ms. Esther answers her saying, "Oh they left with the flicks and the books, and then when they finally left, my husband was ready to have sex. We got in the shower, with the water running, steam was everywhere. He started to caress my breasts up and down and then all over. This process went even further. We played around for a little while longer then we got out of the shower. My husband got some music started the kind we like. I went to the bedroom to get dressed up and putting perfume on, I was getting prepared to be who he wanted me to be that night, not knowing who, until a porno star was shown in a book. This it dawned on me that I had given the good porn away. So I started to think hard until my heart started pounding. I quickly went into pray as to what is my heart is saying. I was asking the Lord what is going on."

Ms. Louise breaks in and asks, "What was wrong?"

Ms. Esther says, "Well my husband asked about the movies that I gave away, but I turned the t.v. to the porn channel, trying to divert his attention about the movies, he liked that. I hated both but that's what he liked."

Ms. Louise says, "Ms Ester if yooooooou, hated porn so much. Why did you go along with the game instead of tell him the truth?"

Ms. Esther replies, "Honey it wasn't that easy. You see he was addicted to porn. This kind of stuff, causes other sexual desires to rise up that you didn't even know was there. It caused me to have to do other things sexually that I didn't like doing, but my husband love to do it. It was a drive for him."

Ms. Louise asks, "So why didn't you just stop and say no?"

Ms. Esther answers her, "Because that was my husband and I was in love with him. Just like you and the other young ladies, who are in love with their spouses or partners. I just didn't feel quite comfortable telling it all in front of the younger ladies, if you know what I mean. They seem like babies to me, they are still wet behind the ears. This stronghold of love that I had for my husband didn't feel right, but I did it anyway. Just like all of you say, love will make you walk on water and through the fire. Love when it comes into your life is very hard to shake off. That's why we got to be very careful not to be love crazy. The last I heard, love is kind, wonderful and love is full of joy. All of these different strongholds aren't love. Baby, its lust and control but never mind me. Woo, I like that color, very peaceful, that's why God said 'my people are destroyed because of the lack of knowledge."

CHAPTER 10
I HAD A BAD FEELING

As she sat there thinking to herself she says, "Let me finish telling you about that day, before the ladies show up for class." Ms. Esther looking worried again, as she changes positions in her chair. Ms. Esther is a good woman of God and loves Ms. Louise to death, but Ms. Louise's situation is making her think about a lot about life in general. She asks herself, why one of her sisters in Christ has to go through a terrible dilemma identical to hers. Ms. Esther prays for comfort as she looks at Ms. Louise frowning and says, "So who are your husband's friends' and why do they make you feel so bad?"

Ms. Louise answers, "There are a lot of woman, and a couple of men. One of the men is his brother and the other one is a co-worker. There is one lady I see all the time in a vision who is supposed to have been my husband's friend."

Ms. Esther replied sarcastically, "I don't believe that is the truth, by a long shot! You can't believe everything you hear, only what you see! So tell me, why didn't you believe they were friends?"

Ms. Louise looks up and turns in her chair, get a little more comfortable. With her hands she adjusts her glasses for a better view and says, "Ms. Esther, if you only knew! I don't even know where to start. . . . . . Well, I'll start from the day I seen him with her and flipped out. I am on my way to my mother's and minding my own business. Mind you now, my husband is supposed to be at work, and I was driving down the street I looked to my left and saw him at one of his relative's house. Curiosity got to me because I thought he was at work and I started to wonder, 'What was he doing there?' So I turned around in the middle of the road and went back to the house, as I turned into the yard people were coming out of the house laughing, joking, and having a good time! I flipped my mind and before anything was said, I was totally out of control and calling the lot of them names that are not even to be repeated in company. All he did was stare at me as I beat him in the chest, I don't know where I got the strength and the courage to do such a thing! He saw the horns on my head. My whole world was torn apart from that day forward and I realized that my husband would never be right. I truly thought I was saved, but that day proved that I still needed a little more pruning in order to handle this situation differently. In reality, I truly wanted to kill both of them. This was on a Saturday evening and he was supposedly to be working, but he was with his girlfriend, the one I had no knowledge of until then. It was a shocking and very emotional moment for me. What's so strange about it, I had a bad feeling it was another woman, I just couldn't put my finger on it. I know one thing for sure, it hurt me a lot worse then and there, more than thinking about it now. It felt like my heart was being cut out my chest and laid on the table for dinner. The bad thing about all this is, my husband was telling me he's not ready for sex and all this time he was getting it from someone else, so he claimed he could not help me. I used to fight temptation on both sides of the fence. Ms. Esther, I was at the point where I didn't know what do. One day it got so bad I found myself crying and pleading to God. Boy I tell you, if you never want sex to call you by your first name, don't run into a husband like mine. Sometimes I just sit and wonder did God really put this man in my life?"

The two ladies stop and prepare themselves roast beef sandwiches and potato salad for lunch. They are both deep in thought about both of their conversations.

CHAPTER 11
THE THRILL IS GONE

They have finished lunch and go to sit in the living room, each with a cup of tea. The clouds are still eminent and the sky is still threatening for more rain.

Ms. Esther sits up and shakes her head as she says, "I didn't know you were going through this dilemma. (She looks at the clock on the wall). Okay honey its 2:00, and those girls still haven't gotten here, maybe they aren't coming today."

Ms. Louise folds her hands against her beautiful blue dress and replies, "They will probably just come to my 5:00-9:00 class. That's what they usually do when they miss the morning class."

Ms. Esther admires the view outside of the weather and replies, "Oh, I didn't know that you had split classes and I just thought it was one class.

Well we know you stay busy through the week."

Ms. Louise says, "Yeah, you best to believe it, with all this weight I'm carrying. This the only way I know how to keep my sanity with myself and God. Guess what my husband said when I told him I needed him?"

Ms. Esther replies nonchalantly, "I can only imagine what he didn't say."

Ms. Louise chuckles and says, "Well he told me to go find someone else to help me because he couldn't. I will never forget what he suggested, it was a slap in the face. We were going to the store on this particular day and it seemed so far away. I felt like a different person sitting in the same car, looking down!"

He asked me, "Don't you have any friends?"

Ms. Esther says angrily, "What friends! I know he didn't go there, Ms. Louise!"

Ms. Louise nods her head and sadly answers, "Yes he did. I was surprised too. I told him 'no I didn't and he even asked me 'what about my church friends, can't they help me'. Oh my God! I felt as my heart was sliced open and all the life was draining right out of me, then and there!

Ms. Esther shockingly says, "Oh my, doesn't he even know that the congregation is mostly females!!!! What is he going to church for, when he did go to church?"

Ms. Louise snorts and replies, "Where does he come off, asking me something like that! Is he trying to tell me to turn to women for my sexual needs? Has he lost it or what? I told him 'we don't go to church for that, at least not me anyway.' Don't you know he stuck his nose up in the air and said, 'Oh really?'"

Ms. Esther shouts, "Stop child! I know he didn't go there with that bull!"

Ms. Louise answers (exhaling), "Yes he did Ms. Esther, I couldn't believe it either. I said to myself, how he could say something so low to his wife."

Ms. Esther shifts in her chair and says, "My child, my child, I don't want to tell you this, but only a man that is not in love could say something so lowly as that. It goes to show that his mind is truly in the gutter and he may not be able to see clear again! The way I see it honey, the thrill is gone. He's getting his freak on with someone else. No need to sugar coat it, I hope you aren't blind to see that either.

Ms Louise says, "Ms. Esther, to tell you the truth, it's too much going on to be blind, stupid, and dumb. It hit me like a ton of bricks. I never would have thought my husband would do me this way!"

Ms. Esther says, "Honey, that husband of yours reminds me of a pimp, they are the only ones that willingly supply women in that way."

Ms. Louise looks at Ms. Esther bitterly and asks, "Are you trying to call me a prostitute?"

Ms. Esther laughs and put her hand on her chest and she says, "No! my child."

Ms. Louise again asks, "Then what are you trying to tell me?"

Ms. Esther replies, "I am saying a pimp will send his prostitute away when he can no longer make money off her. When she is used up and no good any more, he lets her go. All the men have no need for her either, so she becomes a hoe. She has to find another way to make money. She is treated as an outcast and not even allowed to be around the other women and he pimp runs her off the block. He threatens her, that if he ever catches her in or near his area he will make her life a living hell. You may even find her dead in the trash bin or even in an alley. Just remember both the pimp and the hoe, destroy their own souls because of their sin."

Ms. Louise looks up frowning and saying, "I don't understand." Ms. Esther looks at her and says, "Baby, YOU are no good in your husband eyes, and YOU have been replaced!!! There is a hole deep inside and that's what you feel, and why you keep seeing the other woman."

Ms. Louise bows her head into her hands and says, "Oh my God, I feel like crying!

Ms. Esther rubs Ms. Louise's on the back and says, "Baby don't cry, it's his loss and your gain. You haven't slept with him yet, have you?"

Ms. Louise turns and look up at her and boldly says, "I have plenty of sense, that will never happen until I find out the truth, and when I do he's going straight to the clinic.

Ms. Esther says, "Honey take my word for it, when he does open up his eyes, he's going to come crawling back. Just hang in there, God is going to bring you out as pure as gold! Don't worry child. Everything is going to be alright through the power of God!" It has been an extremely long day, and they haven't paid any attention to the time. She looks at the clock and realizes its 4:00, classes are about to begin. "Would you like me to fix something to eat before class starts?"

Ms. Louise looks at the time and exclaims, "Oh my, time flies when you are having fun! Why sure that would be nice, so we can have something to eat. I will cook something else for that man of mine, shoot you know how that goes."

Ms. Esther says, "Yeah, feed him up with kindness. Don't let him see you sweat."

Ms. Louise answers, "What! I was talking about my son, he's my focus and God."

Ms. Esther surprisingly replies, "Well, you are blessed to have that big handsome manas your son, he's very humble and kind. So what are you going to cook for him?"

Ms. Louise happily answers with a smile on her face, "Hmmm, probably some fried chicken, macaroni and cheese, collard greens and a red velvet cake, what do you think?"

Ms. Esther rubs her stomach walking towards the kitchen and says, "Hmm, that sounds good, I'll help you get started. Where are your pots and pans?"

Ms. Louise points and says, "In the right bottom cabinet. You make the cake and macaroni. I'll cook the greens and chicken."

CHAPTER 12
THE TWO SIDES OF THE COIN

They are in the kitchen preparing dinner for them and Ms. Louise's son, while still waiting on the young ladies to arrive.

Ms. Esther asks, "Okay. How do your children feel about all this madness you are going through with your husband?"

Ms. Louise throws her heads sideways and responds with a smile, "Well, they just want what's best for me, but in reality, they think I am a fool to put up with his bull____. You know what? They never let their opinions come between us. I really respect them for that. My son is hilarious, he says one reason I'm still trying is because I don't have any game. Like now, we are separated, men would speak to me and I would respond with an attitude. I guess that's the game I didn't have when I was still with my husband. I tell my children, the reason I don't respond with interest is because, in my heart I rather have my husband more than any other man. I know it sounds crazy, but when you are not the one that is causing the pain, grief, and being the deceptive one. It is very hard to let go of all the real love, romance, and the money, when you are the one always on the wrong side of the coin. There is nothing left to do but hope for a change in you and not the other person. If you are the one on the right side of the coin, you pray for that day your loved one will see you and not their wants. The coin has two sides, one good and one bad, you always hope and pray you come out on the good side. Your soul bleeds for a cure to heal you from listening to those who don't understand and are calling you a fool. Truth be told, it only takes one person to pick up the coin and see the good side. On the side with the man's head, you will see the good side of a person, while on the back side with the building shows the bad side of a person."

They are finished with their dinner and are washing the dishes. They return to the living room with a fresh cup of tea to relax and the conversation continues.

Ms. Esther understandingly replies, "Baby you know what? You're right, it does take someone like us who have been through the kind of situations that we have, in order to understand the good side and the bad side of the coin."

Ms. Louise says, "I tell my children can I pray for the better, because it makes me sick to my stomach to imagine being with another man, but they still tell me I'm crazy to put up with their father. Even though I would still pray to God and ask for his healing."

Ms. Esther looks out the window and shakes her head, and reminisces back to when her husband was still alive. She remembers him as a good man and father, and wonders how a man could put a woman through the hell Louise's husband puts her through. She asks Ms. Louise, "What do you say to the men who speak to you?"

Ms. Louise replies, "Nothing, I'm bitter and sweet and I make it short."

Ms. Esther, "I hear you. You are very wise to even think about starting over."

Ms. Louise laughs, "The thought of being with someone else crossed my mind, but the Lord always stops me in my tracks. I would be fighting temptation and feel I was losing the battle. The only thing that kept me afloat is knowing that God loves me. Oh that devil will come back and say I am going to fail and try to tempt me. How he laughs in my face is by my husband refusing to love me."

Ms. Esther looks away and imagines her life when she was young and remembers it as an experience and worthwhile right time to the end, she then replies, "See Louise, that's what I admire about you. You know God loves you and your praise for him shows."

Ms. Louise stares at Ms. Esther and frowns, saying, "What's so amazing about that?"

Ms. Esther throws up her hands and praises the Lord and then says, "A lot of people like you surrender to temptation and lose everything they got. I will tell you another temptation movement the devil will try to get YOU!!! When you find yourself getting mad at your husband, you may drive by his friend's house just to see if he's there, or call him to find out where he's at. But you may not find the answer, it's called 'curiosity kills the cat'. He knows what you're up to, and when he figures this out, that makes him mad too. With both of you mad, all it does is make it seem like you are being used, which may even cause an argument. Oops, I busted the enemy's bubble as my pastor would say. Yes the devil is a lair in all his tricks he plays. It's the trick of the enemy I tell you. The enemy wants you to fail and fall prey to jealousy and rage. he knows how to get you in these areas and keep you there for a while but not for long when you have God on your side!"

CHAPTER 13

WHERE DID YOU FIND
THE MEANING OF LOVE?

The doorbell rings and they both look up and see that it's time for her class to start. She opens the door and greets Paulina and Keisha with Mimie coming up the walk after them, with a hug and a smile.

The trio enter the room and smile, "Hello everybody, how are you all today?"

Ms. Louise and Ms. Esther say in unison as they walk into the shop, "We are doing fine. How are you all?"

Ms. Esther looks up and sees Mimie's big belly coming towards her and says, "Oh my, look at my precious, she is such a sweetie. I sure will be glad when you have that baby."

Ms. Louise looks behind them and asks, "Where are the other two?" Mimie replies, "Oh they're coming later."

Ms. Esther says, "So it's just you three and the young lady that never says anything. Oh what's her name?"

Mimie says, "You got to be talking about Sara."

Ms. Esther looks over her glasses and says, "Let me tell you all something. You have to keep a close eye on these types of people, you hear me?"

The doorbell rings again. Ms. Louise asks, "Who can this be?" She walks towards the door and asks, "Who is it?"

"It's me, Sara and Sheria, Ms. Louise."

Ms. Esther shakes her head and looks at the door before Ms. Louise opens it, and says "Hmmm, speak of you know who and they show up. That's kind of strange don't you think? By the way, who is Sheria?"

Mimie says, "She was standing outside Ms. Esther, before you started to talk about her."

Ms. Esther replies, "Yeah, believe what you want."

Mimie replies, "No disrespect to you but I won't." Then she changes the subject before Sara enters the room, "It sure does smell good in here Ms. Louise. I hope your cooking enough for all of us. The baby is sure going to love this fried chicken. By the way, where is your husband?" Just at that moment, Paulina, Keisha, Sara and Sheria enter the kitchen, also smelling the aroma of the food.

Sara introduces Sheria to the group, "Hey everyone. This here is Sheria and she is a friend to Joanna, and she is also our new member."

Everyone says, "Hello and welcome to our little sewing group!"

Ms. Louise looks up from the pot and answers Mimie, "We aren't together sweetie, so he won't be coming home today. That's why Ms. Esther is staying with me for a while, so I won't be alone."

Mimie nods and says, "Oh, so she's here to keep you company. Shoot I personally think your husband ain't all there! I don't even know why you put up with him for so long."

Ms. Louise smiles and replies, "I don't, it's something I have adjusted to, I know it's wrong…. but at one time I was so afraid of my husband."

Paulina boastfully says, "You still call this love after all your husband has put you through? I don't call it love! I call it crazy, I call it deception, I call it manipulation, I call it control and must I go on?"

Ms. Louise looks at her and sighs gracefully, "I've learned that love never dies, love will be there for me when I'm down. Love will accept all of my faults and will appreciate me. Love is unconditional, must I say more?" Paulina laughingly replies, "Hmm, where did you find that meaning of love? The last time a man told me he loved me, was when I gave him my phone bill money! Five days later, he showed up with a bag of candy and flowers that he bought with my money, apologizing, and saying, 'Baby, I love you.' Girl for five days I was planning on some way to kill him and say love made me do it!"

Kishia asks her, "So what did you do to him?"

Paulina answers with a smirk, "Oh yeah, I took the candy and the flowers from him. Thank God, the children were going off to school. She leans to one side with her hand planted on her hip and tosses her head to one side and answers with a big smile, "Girl, let me tell you! I called him into the room and made love to him until he fell asleep. I waited awhile and then found some old shoes and took the strings out of them. I tied his hands and feet to the frame of the bed."

Keisha chimes in and comments, "Oh this is sounding good!"

Paulina speaks again, "Then I dialed 911, and told them, they got 5 minutes to come get this good for nothing fool up out of my house or I'll beat the---- out of him!"

Keisha astonished at what she is hearing and answers, "Girl! You called the police!"

Paulina says, "Yes, I love him enough to call the police on myself. In my mind I really wanted to beat the hell out of him before they got there."

Keisha exclaims, "Oh my God, you didn't!"

Paulina heatedly says, "I took off my belt, but I was wishing I had a bat! I started to beat him and he woke up on the first hit startled. I was shouting at him and saying, 'baby, say I love!! Say I love you baby! If you say it I will let you loose!!!' Girl, he was crying, 'I love you baby!! I love you baby!! Yeah! Just what I thought!!!! You won't be taking another woman's money and then show back up days later, telling her 'I love you'!"

Keisha, "Girl, what did the police do to you?"

Paulina proudly answers, "I got charged with assault and battery. They took me to jail."

Ms. Louise, Ms. Esther and Mimie gasp in astonishment and they all comment, "Oh Gosh!!!"

Keisha expresses with her hands and says, "Are you kidding me, to jail?"

Paulina smugly says with a nod of her head, "Yes, to jail! But it was worth every penny! The judge and the whole court thought it was so funny. I told the judge, 'I'm sorry, but I don't play love games.' I was fined $1500.00 and 120 hours community service for the charge. Some People think love is just a word and that they can use it to their advantage. Love will cause you to do crazy things, like having the word 'stupid' written all over your forehead for everyone to see."

Sara quietly, listening to all of the conversations, steps up and asks, "So Paulina, after all you went through with this man and ending up in jail. What do you believe LOVE, really is?"

Paulina is surprised at the question from Sara and haughtily answers, "Love will have you acting like a zombie-blind to what is happening to you, or like a robot-doing things automatically, or slave-doing things when told. When this kind of love is present it's very hard to just say no more, no more."

Sara calmly replies, "This is the kind of love, Ms. Louise has and the reason why she stayed with her husband for so long. He had his sneaky little ways of making her feel like he truly loved her, in time she grew out of it and searched for real love, she found herself through God. The 'real love' she found could see straight through him. She knows when he's lying or when he's were telling the truth."

Ms. Esther knowingly replies, "I told you all to watch them quiet ones! (nodding her head) Uhmmmm, well this young lady seems to have had her share of moments of love in the past."

Sara answers with her head bowed towards the floor, "Yeah I have and it wasn't so pretty."

Paulina answers, "Girl, those seven fools have taught me a lot, when it comes to men."

Sara looks up again after sewing together some pieces and replies, "I have had my share and learned that true love never dies. True love will do whatever it takes to do for there family and mate."

Ms. Louise gets up out of her chair and approaches Sara and joyfully exclaims while hugging her, "Only GOD could have told you that! AMEN!!!"

All the while they are in conversation, they are sewing pieces together and the quilt is half way done. Ms. Louise's son, Dah, comes home.

Dah greets the ladies, "Good evening ladies, how are you all doing?"

Paulina walks toward him and flirtingly says while batting her lashes at him, "It could be better, now that you're here."

Ms. Louise says to Dah, "Sweetheart, your dinner is in the oven." Dah just smiles at her and goes into the kitchen to eat.

All the while they are in conversation, they are sewing pieces together and the quilt is half way done. Ms. Louise's son, Dah, comes home.

Dah greets the ladies, "Good evening ladies, how are you all doing?" Paulina walks toward him and flirtingly says while batting her lashes at him, "It could be better, now that you're here." Ms. Louise says to Dah, "Sweetheart, your dinner is in the oven." Dah just smiles at her and goes into the kitchen to eat.

CHAPTER 14
GETTING TO KNOW SHERIA

Ladies continue with their sewing after their heated conversation on the love subject. The telephone suddenly rings, and startles everyone. Ring ring ring!

Paulina answers, "Hello?"

Joann answers, "Hello, what 'cha all sewing?"

Paulina tells her' "Girl, we are almost finished sewing, class is almost over. We've been waiting on you two, where you all at?"

Joanna replies, "Oh yeah, that's right, it don't seem that late. So everybody is still there?"

Paulina replies, "Yes. All accept you and Kendra."

Joanna asks, "Hey girl, did Ms. Louise cook anything tonight?"

Paulina replies, "Yes she did. She cooked up some good ole' fried chicken, nice, juicy and crispy, along with macaroni and cheese, and a side of collard greens. We also had red velvet cake to top everything off!" Joanna answers enthusiastically, "Wow! That sounds delicious. Man, I can almost taste that good ole' cooking. Jesus girl, please stop, I haven't eaten all day, I just might leave this girl and come eat!"

Paulina suddenly asks, "Hold up now. "Leave who? Kendra?"

Joanna answers, "Yes Kendra."

Paulina asks Joanna, "What do you mean leave her? What are you doing with Kendra?"

Joanna replies' "Oh, I was just admiring the work of God. How he made darkness in the sky, the stars is still in there place, everything is still in its rightful place. Can you imagine what God was thinking at the time? Was he really thinking about little old us."

Paulina answers in puzzlement, "Ok, you are not a rocket scientist. Why are you talking like that?"

Joanna smiling, replies, "Oh girl, it's just a beautiful thing to be able to really have time with God at this moment. I'm just amazed at his work." She then laughs.

Paulina still puzzled at this time answers, "Ok, you know what? You're scaring me 'the old folks used to say, 'When a person is talking very strange, like you are doing? Look out! Something is going to happen.'

Joanna asks frowning, "What are you trying to say?"

Ms. Louise finally asks, "Paulina, honey. Are you still talking to Joanna?"

Paulina says, "Yes, she is talking crazy."

Joanna says, "What? It don't take a rocket scientist to study the creation of God, I'm just pleasantly amazed at this time."

Paulina says, "Ok, whatever Joann!"

Joanna replies, "Girl, did my friend Sheria get there?"

Paulina answers, "Yes, she got here when Sara got here."

Joanna asks, "Can I speak to her?"

Paulina motions to Sheria, "Sheira. Joanna wants to talk to you on the phone."

Sheria answers the phone, "Hello! Hey, I am enjoying myself everybody is so friendly, totally different from work. Girl, I told you that they're great. So how is your husband? Did he get any better? No, he is not."

Joann replies, "What is he going to do about going back to work? Sheria exhales and says, "Girl, I don't even know. He does have health insurance coverage, but if he leaves the company, he will have no coverage. That's all messed up how his job just won t let him return back to work." Joanna replies, "Well girl, my father was just like your husband." Mimie and Paulina asks Sheria, "Are you still talking to Joanna?" Sheria replies, "Yes, she's still waiting on Kendra."

Everybody says, "Ohhhhh, we can't wait 'til you meet Kendra." Sheria says, "Hey girl, I'll talk to you later." Hangs up the phone. Joanna answers, "Okay, later."

Ms. Louise seizes the moment, while standing behind her and asks, "I heard you talking about your husband, is he sick? Baby, is he ok?"

Sheria wearily answers, "Yeah, he's ok. He is getting ready to have another surgery on his leg, there is something going on in his leg vessels. They are trying to save it."

Surprisingly, Ms. Louise says, "According to your information sheet and he's so young to be that sick, but sickness doesn't know age. Sickness is like and stray bullet and can come upon you at the least time you would expect it."

Paulina interrupts and says, "Well honey I hope he is able to pay those high bills."

Sheria answers, "He can handle it for now, he is on short-term disability. We also have some money saved up, I just hope we don't run out, before he gets back to work." She breathes in.

Ms. Louise intercedes, "My God, we just got to pray harder for you and your husbands' strength."

Sheria's phone is ringing, "Oh, I gotta take this call it's my husband." Sheria talking to her husband, "Hello honey, how are you doing? Is everything okay, you don't sound right."

Mr. Paul(Sheria's husband)answers, "Not so good, I got some bad news.

We got a letter in the mail saying we are gonna have to file for bankruptcy."

Sheria moans sadly and asks, "Oh no! Why? How much time are they giving us in order to resolve this?"

Mr. Paul answers, "Honey we were paying them out of my check. The letter says we got one month."

Sheria asks on a more cheerful note, "Let's hope we get your disability back pay. Other than that, how are you?"

Mr. Paul answers her saying, "I'm trying to psych my mind into dealing with this surgery. He changes the subject and asks her, "How do you like you quilting classes?"

Sheria replies, more at ease, "It's great I thank you for letting me have this time."

Mr. Paul says, "I'm glad, I miss you. When are you coming home?

The grandkids are hungry and your daughter doesn't have any gas money."

Sheria moans, "Oh God, tell her to call somebody! I'm not leaving class tonight."

Mr. Paul answers with a snort, "Honey, you know that girl never can hold onto gas money! Besides, I told you a long time ago, to kick those grown, wanna be children, out of our house. You are the only mother eagle I know, who won't push the baby eagles off the cliff, and let them learn how to fly. They are supposed to be taking care of us, not the other way around! They all need to go out on their own."

Sheria says, "Honey, if she calls again, just tell her to find another way home. You know those children can't afford to live out there, on their own. Where are they supposed to get the money?"

Mr Paul replies, "Where do we get the money from?"

Sheria sweetly says, "Honey, don't start with the children today."

Mr. Paul responds, "I'm not, I just want them to leave! Go get them out from around me! Our monthly expense is $3200.00 a month. I'd like to see them pay that some day. Then I will hush."

Sheria says, "Honey, are you through! I love you and I'll see you when I get home."

Mr Paul says, "Ok, but one day you will listen to me about those children. I love you, see you when you get home, and be safe!"

Sheria and Mr. Paul end their conversation and she turns her attention back to the sewing club.

Sheria comments about her husband, "My husband really gets on my nerves about our children."

Sara asks, "Sheria, what's wrong?"

Sheria answers, "My husband is always complaining about money and our children. I will be so glad when he goes back to work."

Sara replies, "Girl you need to stop. Your children are overdue in your home. Your husband is sick. You better thank God he is still here, after all he has been through. Your husband had a sugar level of 865 and high blood pressure at stroke level. Always thank God, he is here for a reason. Money is not everything so don't rush your husband into going back to work so soon."

Sheria says, "But we are at risk of losing everything! Our house, our cars, our credit will be ruined, what else can I add?"

Sara looks at her and says, "Sheria, my mother always told me, God is our everything! If we just believe and have faith, he will surely give it all back and more! Remember he never gives us more than we can handle."

CHAPTER 15
THE BREAK IN

The conversation has shifted to Ms. Louise's store and the ladies are all in wonderment, because some of them don't really know her like Joanna.

Ms. Louise asks, "How is the business coming along."

Sheria surprisingly answers, "Well it's doing fine, we are praying for an increase."

Ms. Louise asks, "Did they ever find those thieves that broke into the store?"

Sheria says, "No, they didn't."

Ms. Louise says, "Honey, they have broken into the store twice since the first break in!"

Sheria asks in wonderment, "Excuse me, if I may ask. How did you know about the break in?"

Ms. Louise responds, "I seen it on the news and Joanna also told me about it."

Sheira says, "Yeah, you heard right."

Everyone talks at once in response to this new information of their new club member.

Well, we sure didn't know it was your shop that was robbed! They only showed your husband and not you. We never thought we'd ever get to meet you in person.

Ms. Esther approaches her, touches her on the arm and sorrowfully says, "We are very sorry to hear about your dilemma. Don't worry anymore, for you are among friends and if you ever need to talk or a shoulder to lean on, we are here.'

Sheria tearfully responds to this unexpected support, "Oh, thank you so much! I do need a shoulder or an ear every now and then."

Ms. Louise encouragingly says, "Child, that's why you should keep coming to the sewing club except when your husband gets sick. We will pray that you have no more robberies."

Sheria replies, sadly, "Ms. Louise, I would've come two weeks ago but I didn't have the money to come to class because my husband got sick.

Ms. Louise tells her, "It's not all about the money, darling. Always remember it's all about, 'Reap What You Sew Quilting.' Baby, every quilt you sew will go to somebody like you. who don't have money, who were burned out of their home, who have loved ones in the rest home, there is always someone in need of a quilt. I will always remember where God has brought me out of. I always ask God to never let me get too proud. The more money I make, the more I want to help someone that is in need. I get joy when I think about what God has done for me. Look around you, all of these quilts will bring joy to somebody's life. Just like our God provides for all of us. We should never let the money run our lives. You have that store now make the money and don't forget about the reason God gave you that business. You have a clothing store that business is somebody's blessing so that you have the opportunity to serve a lot of people. God said he will put clothes on our back and shoes on our feet, God is going to send some of customers in there that will not even have a dime. You are Gods' distribution center I feel like preaching but back to that robbery."

Sheria comfortably answers, "My, I love hearing you talk about God, this is the reason why I came. When we were robbed they stole almost the whole men's clothing department. Kays Jays Fashions' loss was $5,500.00. They broke the glass doors with bricks and iron bars. After the robbery, we had to upgrade the insurance policy for the store. We installed security bars on all the windows and also installed surveillance cameras in order for the insurance company to pay for the loss and the damages.

Ms. Louise replies, "They won't get away with that, God don't like ugly."

Sheria says, "The only thing I don't like about owning a store, is when these robberies happen, there is not one glass shop open. Our life is in harm's' way. We lose a lot of sleep watching the store and it is very scary. We sleep with one eye open and one eye closed."

Mimie stops sewing and replies, "Oh my God! You and Miss. Louise are in harm's' way by owning a business. These people don't realize, y'all put your life savings in these businesses."

Shaira angrily responds, "From the looks of it all, a thief is a thief, and your hard earned money and your life is in their hands because it doesn't belong to them! A thief doesn't know nobody but what they are trying to get."

Ms. Esther immediately says, "We are going to have to pray for these business, so that God will put a hedge of protection around them.

Phone rings again and the caller's identity shows up on the T.V. screen. Joanna is calling.

Everyone is surprised and Paulina goes to answer the phone call.

AUTHOR BIOGRAPHY

Betty Jones Married to her handsome husband Shep Jones, who's been her motivator, best friend and lover for 39 years. They have 6 children 21 grandchildren, 17 great grandchildren and counting.

I have written and published one Play for children. Call Lord save my children following many more to come.

My first book series Sex Love Money and then God was written from all the life issue that I have experience with my marriage life. Following a form of a novel story of different woman, mothers, fathers, sisters, brothers and friends . Somebody has experience these issues in life. The life story that all the families is going throw, I lived it day in my marriage and life each day ,month or year my life play out as if it would never end. As a result drama day after day, it was an issue involving the contents of my book Sex Love Money and then God.

People ask me today why did I mention god last. My answer, when do we ever put God first. Henceforth I am so grateful that God is the center, first and last in my life. Because know when these issue comes about I can handle them a lot more with God.

As a result when I begin creative writing of my first book Sex Love Money and then God. In the beginning of my writing I only knew how to write the book and not type. There for it took a long time to type the manuscript out. But my context can from the life experiences of each word. All the while as I write the story of my life into fictional the character voice and names got very strong and intense in the book.

Henceforth after writing this book, is a five part series following the issues in our relationships how we should handle them in a Godly matter and not our own.

www.ingramcontent.com/pod-product-compliance
Lightning Source LLC
Chambersburg PA
CBHW022120050726

47591CB00002B/864